Guest Book to Celebrate:

_____

Guest Name(s) & Relationship To Graduate:

_____

_____

Why I am/we are proud of you:

_____

_____

_____

_____

Words of inspiration for the future:

_____

_____

_____

_____

Guest Name(s) & Relationship To Graduate:

_____

_____

Why I am/we are proud of you:

_____

_____

_____

_____

Words of inspiration for the future:

_____

_____

_____

_____

Guest Name(s) & Relationship To Graduate:

_____

_____

Why I am/we are proud of you:

_____

_____

_____

_____

Words of inspiration for the future:

_____

_____

_____

_____

Guest Name(s) & Relationship To Graduate:

_____

_____

Why I am/we are proud of you:

_____

_____

_____

_____

Words of inspiration for the future:

_____

_____

_____

_____

Guest Name(s) & Relationship To Graduate:

_____

_____

Why I am/we are proud of you:

_____

_____

_____

_____

Words of inspiration for the future:

_____

_____

_____

_____

Guest Name(s) & Relationship To Graduate:

_____

_____

Why I am/we are proud of you:

_____

_____

_____

_____

Words of inspiration for the future:

_____

_____

_____

_____

Guest Name(s) & Relationship To Graduate:

_____

_____

Why I am/we are proud of you:

_____

_____

_____

_____

Words of inspiration for the future:

_____

_____

_____

_____

Guest Name(s) & Relationship To Graduate:

_____

_____

Why I am/we are proud of you:

_____

_____

_____

_____

Words of inspiration for the future:

_____

_____

_____

_____

Guest Name(s) & Relationship To Graduate:

_____

_____

Why I am/we are proud of you:

_____

_____

_____

_____

Words of inspiration for the future:

_____

_____

_____

_____

Guest Name(s) & Relationship To Graduate:

_____

_____

Why I am/we are proud of you:

_____

_____

_____

_____

Words of inspiration for the future:

_____

_____

_____

_____

Guest Name(s) & Relationship To Graduate:

_____

_____

Why I am/we are proud of you:

_____

_____

_____

_____

Words of inspiration for the future:

_____

_____

_____

_____

Guest Name(s) & Relationship To Graduate:

_____

_____

Why I am/we are proud of you:

_____

_____

_____

_____

Words of inspiration for the future:

_____

_____

_____

_____

Guest Name(s) & Relationship To Graduate:

_____

_____

Why I am/we are proud of you:

_____

_____

_____

_____

Words of inspiration for the future:

_____

_____

_____

_____

Guest Name(s) & Relationship To Graduate:

_____

_____

Why I am/we are proud of you:

_____

_____

_____

_____

Words of inspiration for the future:

_____

_____

_____

_____

Guest Name(s) & Relationship To Graduate:

_____

_____

Why I am/we are proud of you:

_____

_____

_____

_____

Words of inspiration for the future:

_____

_____

_____

_____

Guest Name(s) & Relationship To Graduate:

_____

_____

Why I am/we are proud of you:

_____

_____

_____

_____

_____

Words of inspiration for the future:

_____

_____

_____

_____

Guest Name(s) & Relationship To Graduate:

_____

_____

Why I am/we are proud of you:

_____

_____

_____

_____

Words of inspiration for the future:

_____

_____

_____

_____

Guest Name(s) & Relationship To Graduate:

_____

_____

Why I am/we are proud of you:

_____

_____

_____

_____

Words of inspiration for the future:

_____

_____

_____

_____

Guest Name(s) & Relationship To Graduate:

_____

_____

Why I am/we are proud of you:

_____

_____

_____

_____

Words of inspiration for the future:

_____

_____

_____

_____

Guest Name(s) & Relationship To Graduate:

_____

_____

Why I am/we are proud of you:

_____

_____

_____

_____

Words of inspiration for the future:

_____

_____

_____

_____

Guest Name(s) & Relationship To Graduate:

_____

_____

Why I am/we are proud of you:

_____

_____

_____

_____

_____

Words of inspiration for the future:

_____

_____

_____

_____

Guest Name(s) & Relationship To Graduate:

_____

_____

Why I am/we are proud of you:

_____

_____

_____

_____

Words of inspiration for the future:

_____

_____

_____

_____

Guest Name(s) & Relationship To Graduate:

_____

_____

Why I am/we are proud of you:

_____

_____

_____

_____

Words of inspiration for the future:

_____

_____

_____

_____

Guest Name(s) & Relationship To Graduate:

_____

_____

Why I am/we are proud of you:

_____

_____

_____

_____

_____

Words of inspiration for the future:

_____

_____

_____

_____

Guest Name(s) & Relationship To Graduate:

_____

_____

Why I am/we are proud of you:

_____

_____

_____

_____

Words of inspiration for the future:

_____

_____

_____

_____

Guest Name(s) & Relationship To Graduate:

_____

_____

Why I am/we are proud of you:

_____

_____

_____

_____

Words of inspiration for the future:

_____

_____

_____

_____

Guest Name(s) & Relationship To Graduate:

_____

_____

Why I am/we are proud of you:

_____

_____

_____

_____

Words of inspiration for the future:

_____

_____

_____

_____

Guest Name(s) & Relationship To Graduate:

_____

_____

Why I am/we are proud of you:

_____

_____

_____

_____

Words of inspiration for the future:

_____

_____

_____

_____

Guest Name(s) & Relationship To Graduate:

_____

_____

Why I am/we are proud of you:

_____

_____

_____

_____

Words of inspiration for the future:

_____

_____

_____

_____

Guest Name(s) & Relationship To Graduate:

_____

_____

Why I am/we are proud of you:

_____

_____

_____

_____

Words of inspiration for the future:

_____

_____

_____

_____

Guest Name(s) & Relationship To Graduate:

_____

_____

Why I am/we are proud of you:

_____

_____

_____

_____

Words of inspiration for the future:

_____

_____

_____

_____

Guest Name(s) & Relationship To Graduate:

_____

_____

Why I am/we are proud of you:

_____

_____

_____

_____

_____

Words of inspiration for the future:

_____

_____

_____

_____

Guest Name(s) & Relationship To Graduate:

_____

_____

Why I am/we are proud of you:

_____

_____

_____

_____

Words of inspiration for the future:

_____

_____

_____

_____

Guest Name(s) & Relationship To Graduate:

_____

_____

Why I am/we are proud of you:

_____

_____

_____

_____

Words of inspiration for the future:

_____

_____

_____

_____

Guest Name(s) & Relationship To Graduate:

_____

_____

Why I am/we are proud of you:

_____

_____

_____

_____

Words of inspiration for the future:

_____

_____

_____

_____

Guest Name(s) & Relationship To Graduate:

_____

_____

Why I am/we are proud of you:

_____

_____

_____

_____

_____

Words of inspiration for the future:

_____

_____

_____

_____

Guest Name(s) & Relationship To Graduate:

_____

_____

Why I am/we are proud of you:

_____

_____

_____

_____

Words of inspiration for the future:

_____

_____

_____

_____

Guest Name(s) & Relationship To Graduate:

_____

_____

Why I am/we are proud of you:

_____

_____

_____

_____

Words of inspiration for the future:

_____

_____

_____

_____

Guest Name(s) & Relationship To Graduate:

_____

_____

Why I am/we are proud of you:

_____

_____

_____

_____

Words of inspiration for the future:

_____

_____

_____

_____

Guest Name(s) & Relationship To Graduate:

_____

_____

Why I am/we are proud of you:

_____

_____

_____

_____

Words of inspiration for the future:

_____

_____

_____

_____

Guest Name(s) & Relationship To Graduate:

_____

_____

Why I am/we are proud of you:

_____

_____

_____

_____

Words of inspiration for the future:

_____

_____

_____

_____

Guest Name(s) & Relationship To Graduate:

_____

_____

Why I am/we are proud of you:

_____

_____

_____

_____

_____

Words of inspiration for the future:

_____

_____

_____

_____

_____

Guest Name(s) & Relationship To Graduate:

_____

_____

Why I am/we are proud of you:

_____

_____

_____

_____

Words of inspiration for the future:

_____

_____

_____

_____

Guest Name(s) & Relationship To Graduate:

_____

_____

Why I am/we are proud of you:

_____

_____

_____

_____

Words of inspiration for the future:

_____

_____

_____

_____

Guest Name(s) & Relationship To Graduate:

_____

_____

Why I am/we are proud of you:

_____

_____

_____

_____

Words of inspiration for the future:

_____

_____

_____

_____

Guest Name(s) & Relationship To Graduate:

_____

_____

Why I am/we are proud of you:

_____

_____

_____

_____

Words of inspiration for the future:

_____

_____

_____

_____

Guest Name(s) & Relationship To Graduate:

_____

_____

Why I am/we are proud of you:

_____

_____

_____

_____

Words of inspiration for the future:

_____

_____

_____

_____

Guest Name(s) & Relationship To Graduate:

_____

_____

Why I am/we are proud of you:

_____

_____

_____

_____

Words of inspiration for the future:

_____

_____

_____

_____

Guest Name(s) & Relationship To Graduate:

_____

_____

Why I am/we are proud of you:

_____

_____

_____

_____

Words of inspiration for the future:

_____

_____

_____

_____

Guest Name(s) & Relationship To Graduate:

_____

_____

Why I am/we are proud of you:

_____

_____

_____

_____

Words of inspiration for the future:

_____

_____

_____

_____

Guest Name(s) & Relationship To Graduate:

_____

_____

Why I am/we are proud of you:

_____

_____

_____

_____

Words of inspiration for the future:

_____

_____

_____

_____

Guest Name(s) & Relationship To Graduate:

_____

_____

Why I am/we are proud of you:

_____

_____

_____

_____

Words of inspiration for the future:

_____

_____

_____

_____

Guest Name(s) & Relationship To Graduate:

_____

_____

Why I am/we are proud of you:

_____

_____

_____

_____

_____

Words of inspiration for the future:

_____

_____

_____

_____

Guest Name(s) & Relationship To Graduate:

_____

_____

Why I am/we are proud of you:

_____

_____

_____

_____

Words of inspiration for the future:

_____

_____

_____

_____

Guest Name(s) & Relationship To Graduate:

_____

_____

Why I am/we are proud of you:

_____

_____

_____

_____

Words of inspiration for the future:

_____

_____

_____

_____

Guest Name(s) & Relationship To Graduate:

_____

_____

Why I am/we are proud of you:

_____

_____

_____

_____

Words of inspiration for the future:

_____

_____

_____

_____

Guest Name(s) & Relationship To Graduate:

_____

_____

Why I am/we are proud of you:

_____

_____

_____

_____

Words of inspiration for the future:

_____

_____

_____

_____

Guest Name(s) & Relationship To Graduate:

_____

_____

Why I am/we are proud of you:

_____

_____

_____

_____

Words of inspiration for the future:

_____

_____

_____

_____

Guest Name(s) & Relationship To Graduate:

_____

_____

Why I am/we are proud of you:

_____

_____

_____

_____

Words of inspiration for the future:

_____

_____

_____

_____

Guest Name(s) & Relationship To Graduate:

_____

_____

Why I am/we are proud of you:

_____

_____

_____

_____

Words of inspiration for the future:

_____

_____

_____

_____

Guest Name(s) & Relationship To Graduate:

_____

_____

Why I am/we are proud of you:

_____

_____

_____

_____

Words of inspiration for the future:

_____

_____

_____

_____

Guest Name(s) & Relationship To Graduate:

_____

_____

Why I am/we are proud of you:

_____

_____

_____

_____

Words of inspiration for the future:

_____

_____

_____

_____

Guest Name(s) & Relationship To Graduate:

_____

_____

Why I am/we are proud of you:

_____

_____

_____

_____

Words of inspiration for the future:

_____

_____

_____

_____

Guest Name(s) & Relationship To Graduate:

_____

_____

Why I am/we are proud of you:

_____

_____

_____

_____

Words of inspiration for the future:

_____

_____

_____

_____

Guest Name(s) & Relationship To Graduate:

_____

_____

Why I am/we are proud of you:

_____

_____

_____

_____

_____

Words of inspiration for the future:

_____

_____

_____

_____

Guest Name(s) & Relationship To Graduate:

_____

_____

Why I am/we are proud of you:

_____

_____

_____

_____

Words of inspiration for the future:

_____

_____

_____

_____

Guest Name(s) & Relationship To Graduate:

_____

_____

Why I am/we are proud of you:

_____

_____

_____

_____

Words of inspiration for the future:

_____

_____

_____

_____

Guest Name(s) & Relationship To Graduate:

_____

_____

Why I am/we are proud of you:

_____

_____

_____

_____

Words of inspiration for the future:

_____

_____

_____

_____

Guest Name(s) & Relationship To Graduate:

_____

_____

Why I am/we are proud of you:

_____

_____

_____

_____

_____

Words of inspiration for the future:

_____

_____

_____

_____

Guest Name(s) & Relationship To Graduate:

_____

_____

Why I am/we are proud of you:

_____

_____

_____

_____

Words of inspiration for the future:

_____

_____

_____

_____

Guest Name(s) & Relationship To Graduate:

_____

_____

Why I am/we are proud of you:

_____

_____

_____

_____

Words of inspiration for the future:

_____

_____

_____

_____

Guest Name(s) & Relationship To Graduate:

_____

_____

Why I am/we are proud of you:

_____

_____

_____

_____

Words of inspiration for the future:

_____

_____

_____

_____

Guest Name(s) & Relationship To Graduate:

_____

_____

Why I am/we are proud of you:

_____

_____

_____

_____

Words of inspiration for the future:

_____

_____

_____

_____

Guest Name(s) & Relationship To Graduate:

_____

_____

Why I am/we are proud of you:

_____

_____

_____

_____

Words of inspiration for the future:

_____

_____

_____

_____

Guest Name(s) & Relationship To Graduate:

_____

_____

Why I am/we are proud of you:

_____

_____

_____

_____

Words of inspiration for the future:

_____

_____

_____

_____

Guest Name(s) & Relationship To Graduate:

_____

_____

Why I am/we are proud of you:

_____

_____

_____

_____

Words of inspiration for the future:

_____

_____

_____

_____

Guest Name(s) & Relationship To Graduate:

_____

_____

Why I am/we are proud of you:

_____

_____

_____

_____

Words of inspiration for the future:

_____

_____

_____

_____

Guest Name(s) & Relationship To Graduate:

_____

_____

Why I am/we are proud of you:

_____

_____

_____

_____

Words of inspiration for the future:

_____

_____

_____

_____

Guest Name(s) & Relationship To Graduate:

_____

_____

Why I am/we are proud of you:

_____

_____

_____

_____

_____

Words of inspiration for the future:

_____

_____

_____

_____

Guest Name(s) & Relationship To Graduate:

_____

_____

Why I am/we are proud of you:

_____

_____

_____

_____

Words of inspiration for the future:

_____

_____

_____

_____

Guest Name(s) & Relationship To Graduate:

_____

_____

Why I am/we are proud of you:

_____

_____

_____

_____

Words of inspiration for the future:

_____

_____

_____

_____

Guest Name(s) & Relationship To Graduate:

_____

_____

Why I am/we are proud of you:

_____

_____

_____

_____

Words of inspiration for the future:

_____

_____

_____

_____

Guest Name(s) & Relationship To Graduate:

_____

_____

Why I am/we are proud of you:

_____

_____

_____

_____

Words of inspiration for the future:

_____

_____

_____

_____

Guest Name(s) & Relationship To Graduate:

_____

_____

Why I am/we are proud of you:

_____

_____

_____

_____

Words of inspiration for the future:

_____

_____

_____

_____

Guest Name(s) & Relationship To Graduate:

_____

_____

Why I am/we are proud of you:

_____

_____

_____

_____

_____

Words of inspiration for the future:

_____

_____

_____

_____

Guest Name(s) & Relationship To Graduate:

_____

_____

Why I am/we are proud of you:

_____

_____

_____

_____

Words of inspiration for the future:

_____

_____

_____

_____

Guest Name(s) & Relationship To Graduate:

_____

_____

Why I am/we are proud of you:

_____

_____

_____

_____

Words of inspiration for the future:

_____

_____

_____

_____

Guest Name(s) & Relationship To Graduate:

_____

_____

Why I am/we are proud of you:

_____

_____

_____

_____

_____

Words of inspiration for the future:

_____

_____

_____

_____

Guest Name(s) & Relationship To Graduate:

_____

_____

Why I am/we are proud of you:

_____

_____

_____

_____

Words of inspiration for the future:

_____

_____

_____

_____

Guest Name(s) & Relationship To Graduate:

_____

_____

Why I am/we are proud of you:

_____

_____

_____

_____

_____

Words of inspiration for the future:

_____

_____

_____

_____

_____

Guest Name(s) & Relationship To Graduate:

_____

_____

Why I am/we are proud of you:

_____

_____

_____

_____

Words of inspiration for the future:

_____

_____

_____

_____

Guest Name(s) & Relationship To Graduate:

_____

_____

Why I am/we are proud of you:

_____

_____

_____

_____

Words of inspiration for the future:

_____

_____

_____

_____

Gift Log

Guest   Gift

_____   _____

_____   _____

_____   _____

_____   _____

_____   _____

_____   _____

_____   _____

_____   _____

Gift Log

Guest	Gift
_____	_____
_____	_____
_____	_____
_____	_____
_____	_____
_____	_____
_____	_____
_____	_____

Gift Log

Guest	Gift
_____	_____
_____	_____
_____	_____
_____	_____
_____	_____
_____	_____
_____	_____

Gift Log

Guest	Gift
_____	_____
_____	_____
_____	_____
_____	_____
_____	_____
_____	_____
_____	_____

Gift Log

Guest	Gift

Gift Log

Guest   ### Gift

_____   _____

_____   _____

_____   _____

_____   _____

_____   _____

_____   _____

_____   _____

Gift Log

Guest	Gift

Gift Log

Guest	Gift
_____	_____
_____	_____
_____	_____
_____	_____
_____	_____
_____	_____
_____	_____

Made in the USA
Monee, IL
13 July 2020